Christmas Songs for Accordion

Arranged by GARY MEISNER

CONTENTS

HAL•LEONARD®
CORPORATION

7777 W. BLUEMOUND RD. P.O. BOX 13819 MILWAUKEE, WI 53213

T0050969

Blue Christmas

Words and Music by
Billy Hayes and Jay Johnson

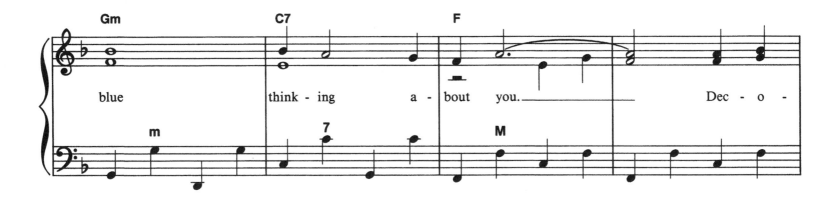

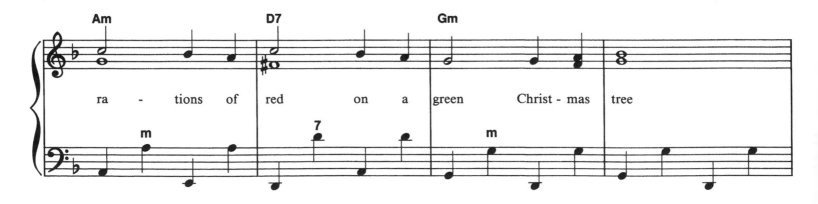

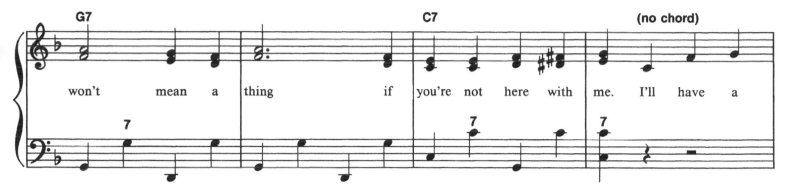

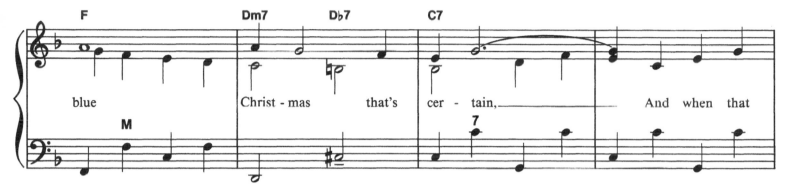

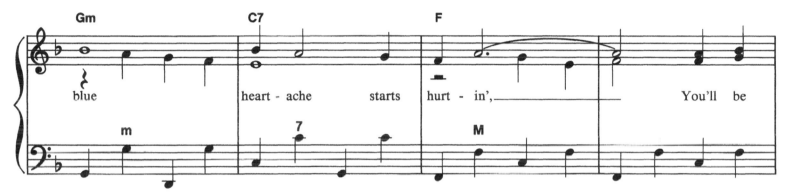

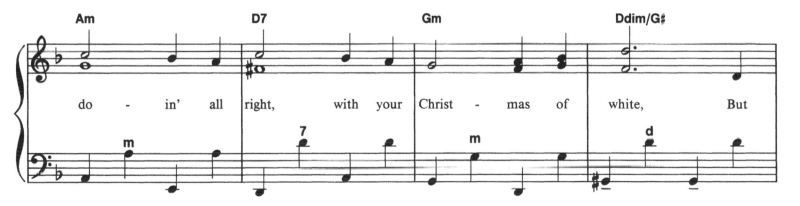

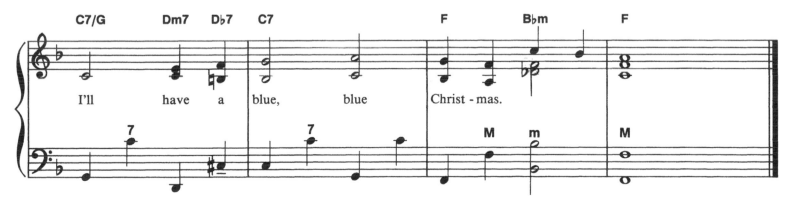

The Chipmunk Song

Words and Music by
Ross Bagdasarian

5

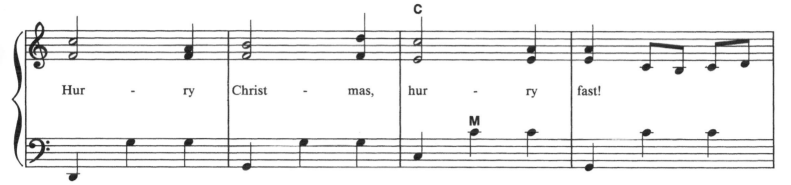

Hur - ry Christ - mas, hur - ry fast!

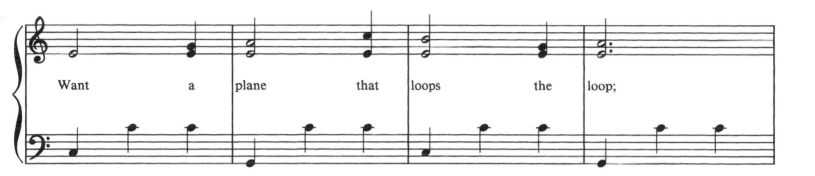

Want a plane that loops the loop;

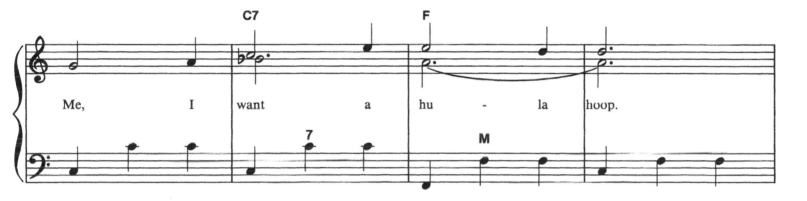

Me, I want a hu - la hoop.

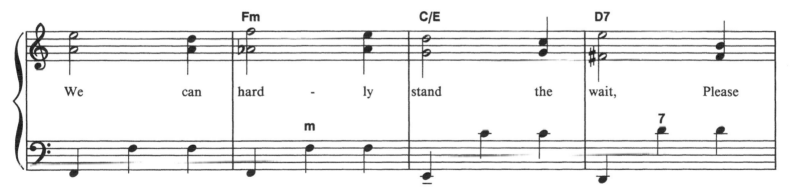

We can hard - ly stand the wait, Please

Christ - mas don't be late.

The Christmas Waltz

Lyric by Sammy Cahn
Music by Jule Styne

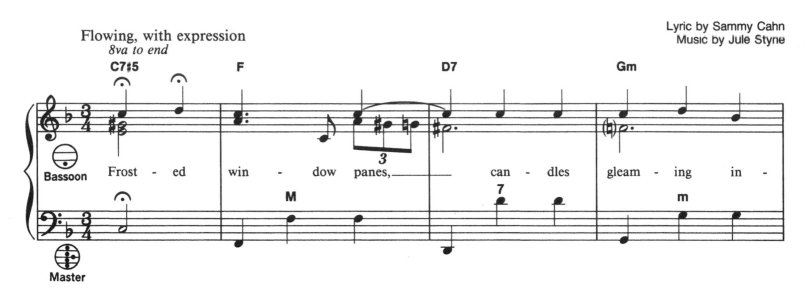

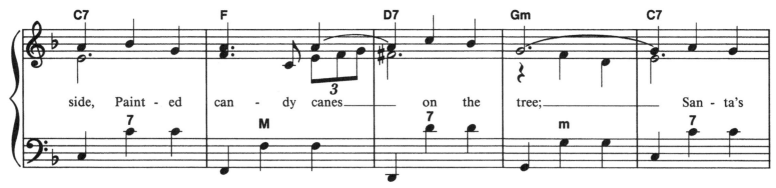

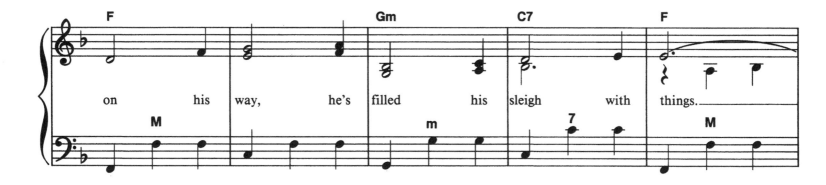

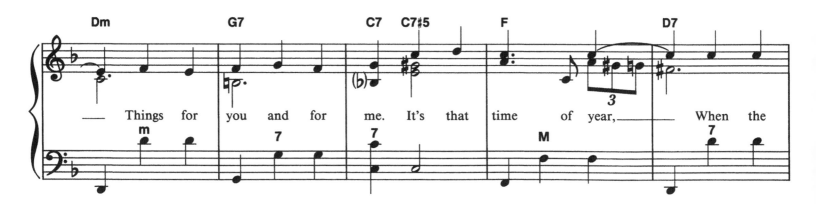

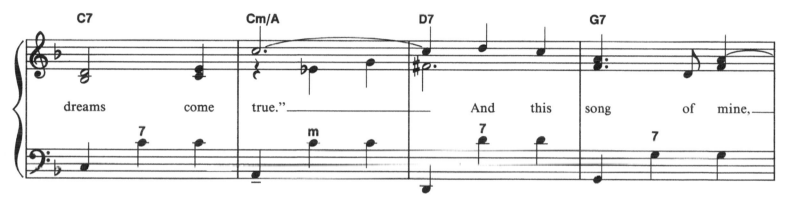

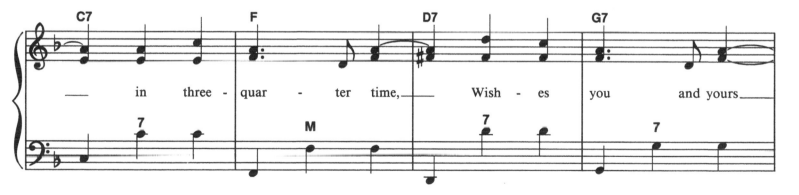

Frosty The Snow Man

Words and Music by
Steve Nelson and Jack Rollins

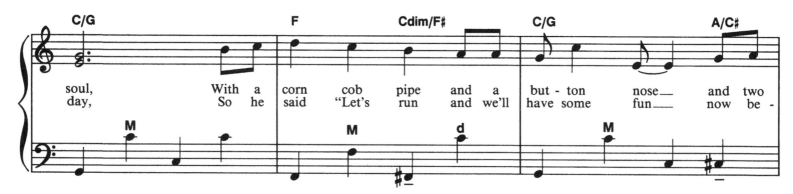

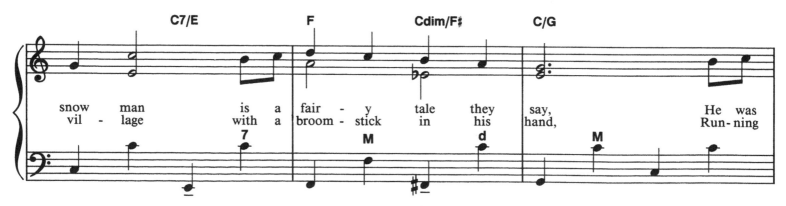

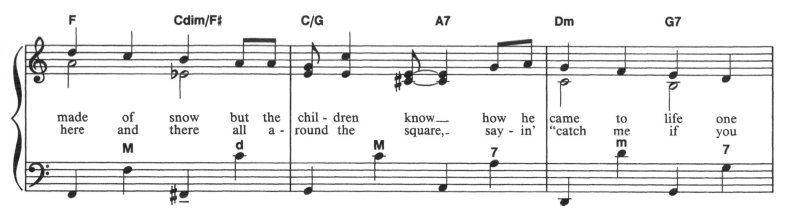

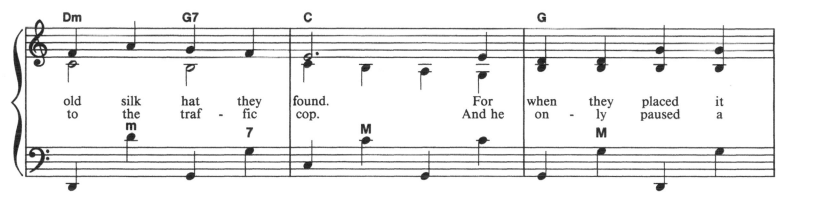

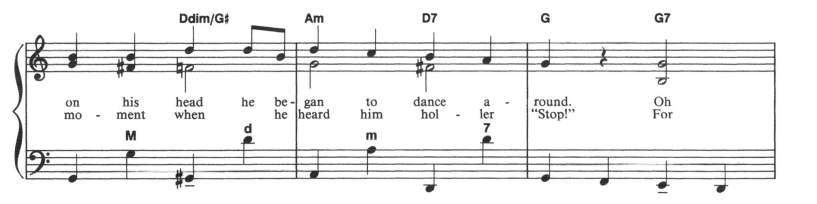

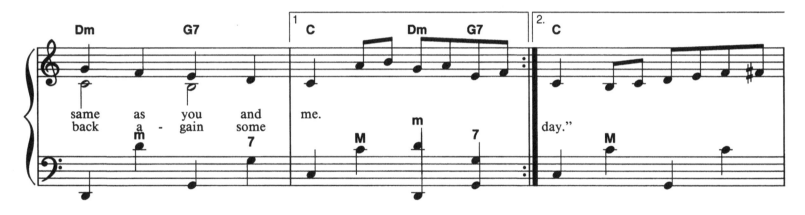

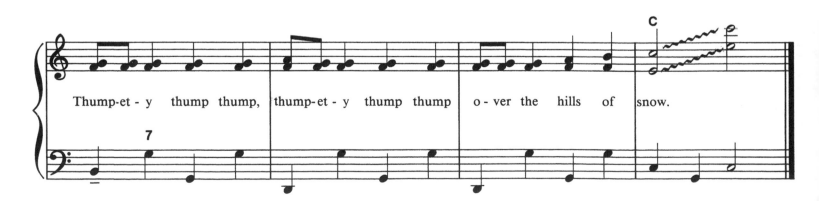

A Holly Jolly Christmas

Words and Music by
Johnny Marks

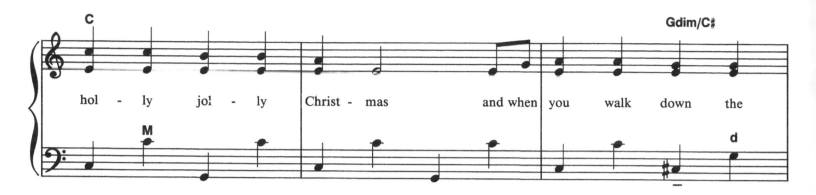

kiss her once for me. Have a hol - ly jol - ly

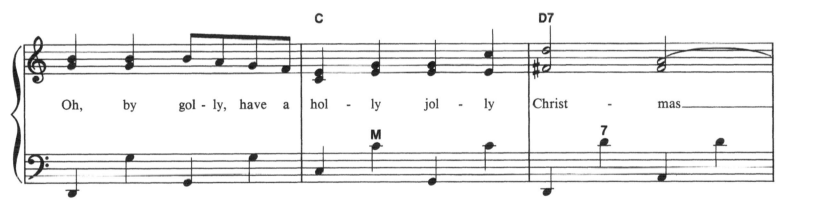

Christ - mas, and in case you did - n't hear

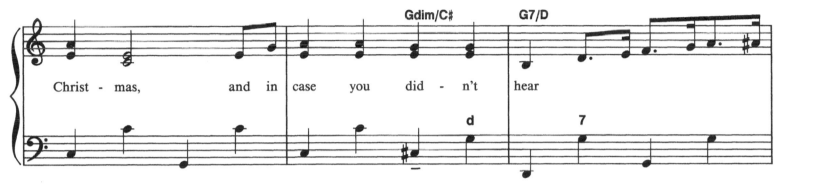

Oh, by gol - ly, have a hol - ly jol - ly Christ - mas

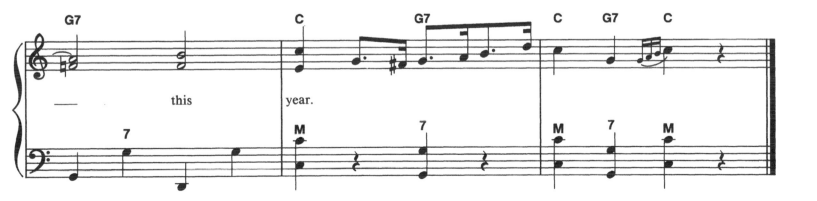

this year.

(There's No Place Like)
Home For The Holidays

Words by Al Stillman
Music by Robert Allen

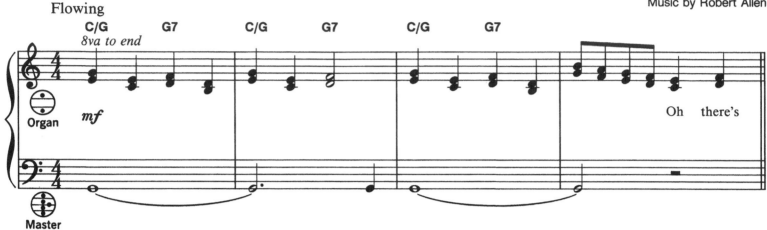

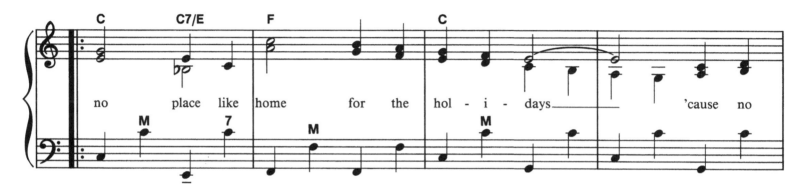

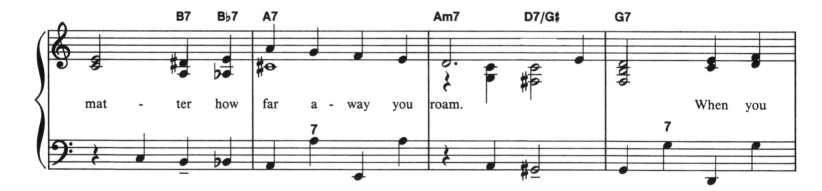

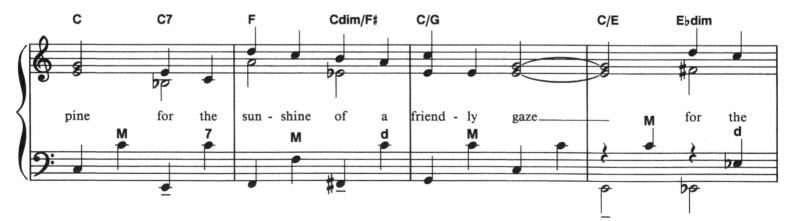

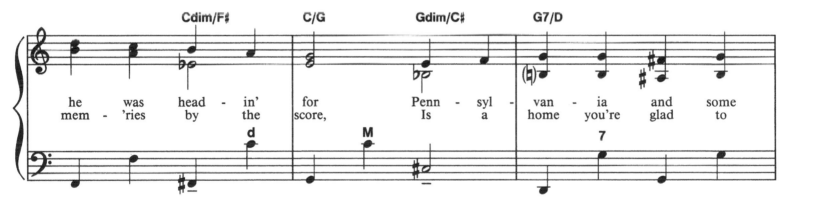

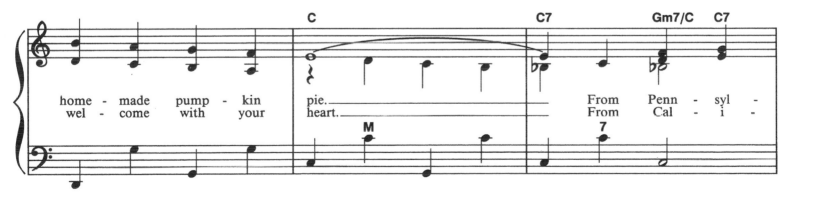

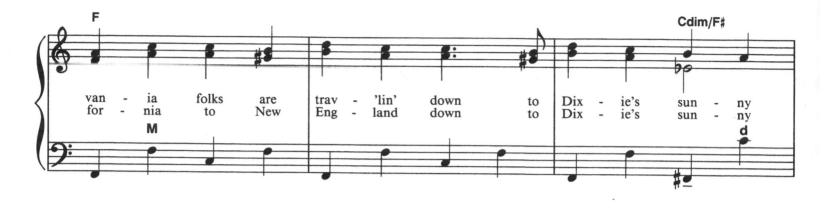

van - ia folks are trav - 'lin' down to Dix - ie's sun - ny
for - nia to to New Eng - land down to Dix - ie's sun - ny

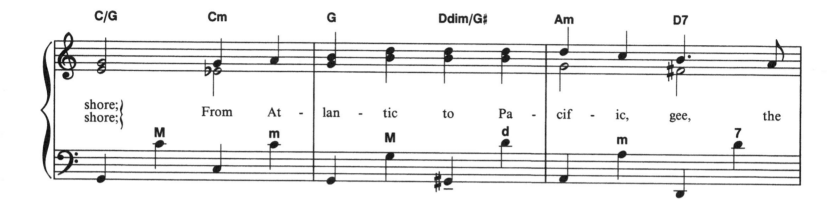

shore;) From At - lan - tic to Pa - cif - ic, gee, the
shore;}

traf - fic is ter - ri - fic. Oh, there's no place like

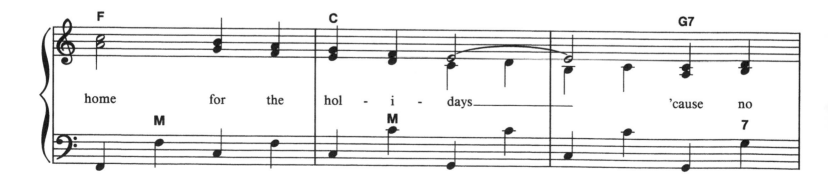

home for the hol - i - days_____ 'cause no

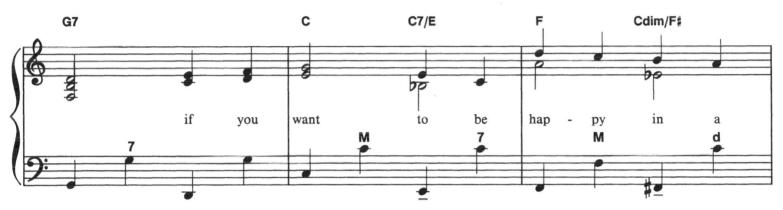

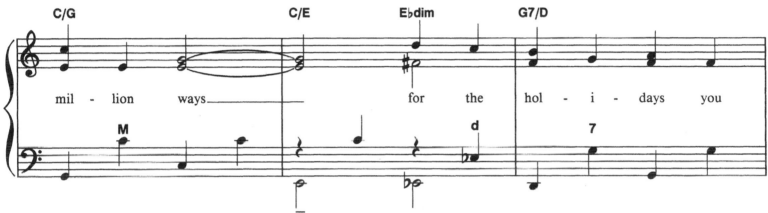

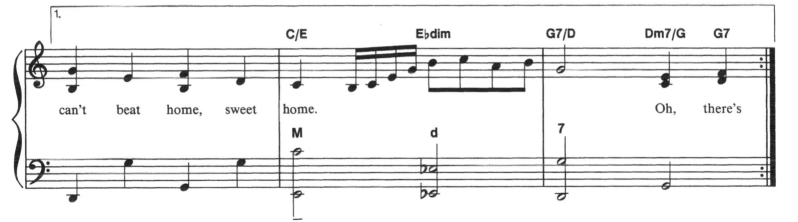

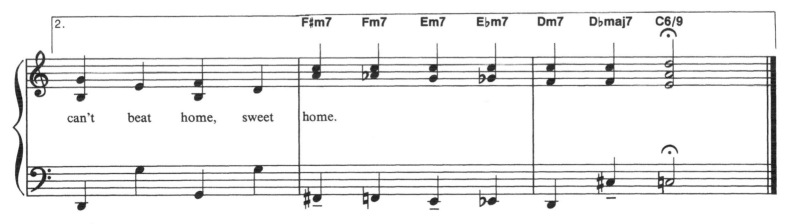

I Saw Mommy Kissing Santa Claus

Words and Music by
Tommie Connor

Moderately slow

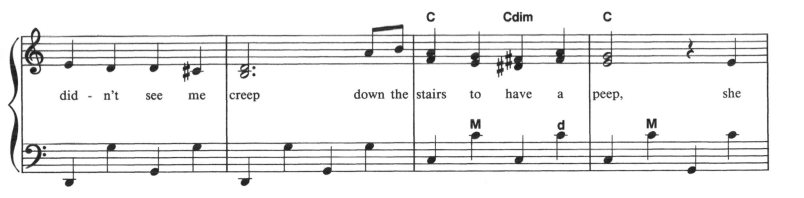

did - n't see me creep down the stairs to have a peep, she

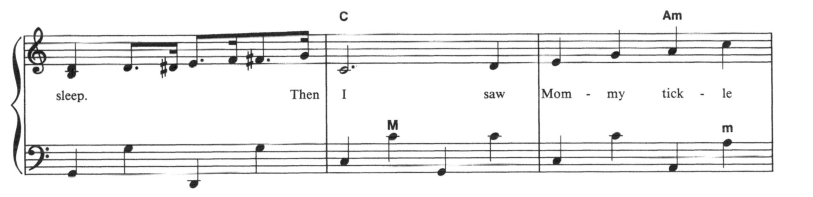

thought that I was tucked up in my bed - room fast a -

sleep. Then I saw Mom - my tick - le

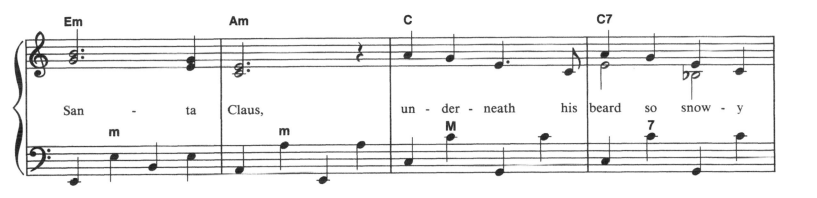

San - ta Claus, un - der - neath his beard so snow - y

white. _____ Oh, what a laugh it would have

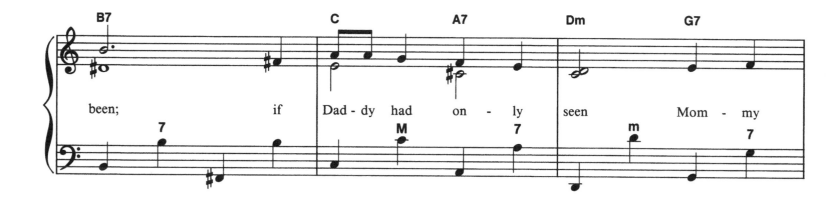

been; if Dad - dy had on - ly seen Mom - my

kiss - ing San - ta Claus last night.

night.

Jingle-Bell Rock

Words and Music by
Joe Beal and Jim Boothe

bush - els of fun
Jin - gle - bell Square

Now the jin - gle - hop has be - gun.___

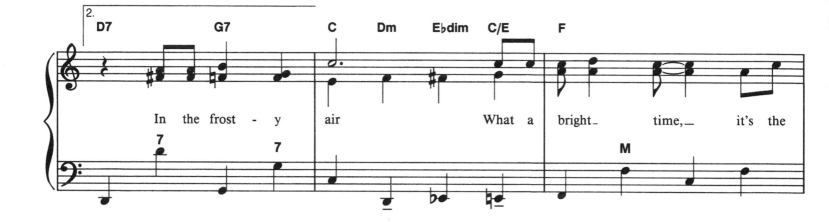

In the frost - y air

What a bright___ time,___ it's the

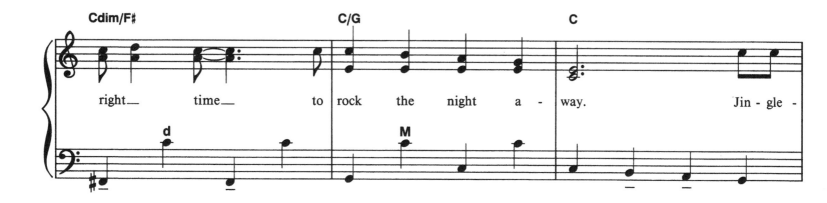

right___ time___ to rock the night a - way.

Jin - gle -

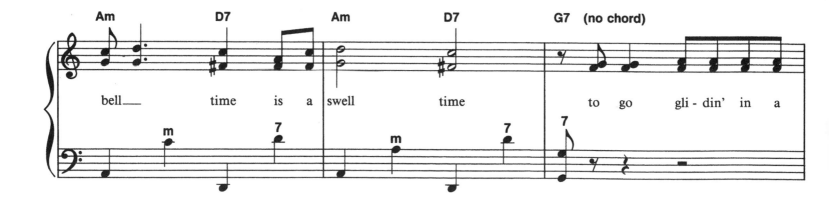

bell___ time is a swell time

to go gli - din' in a

one-horse sleigh— Gid - dy - ap, jin - gle horse pick up your feet.—

Jin - gle a - round the clock. Mix and min - gle in a

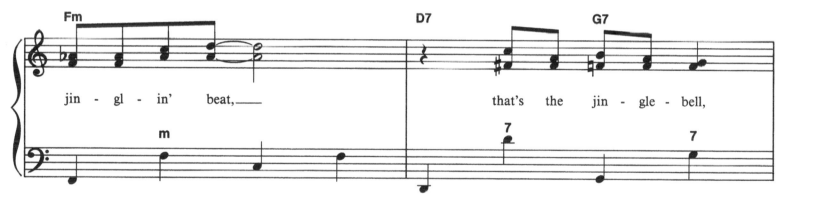

jin - gl - in' beat,— that's the jin - gle- bell,

that's the jin - gle- bell, that's the jin - gle- bell rock.

I'll Be Home For Christmas

Lyrics by Kim Gannon
Music by Walter Kent

Moderately slow

Lyrics:
I'll be home for Christ-mas

You can count on me.

Please have snow and mis-tle-toe And

pres-ents on the tree.

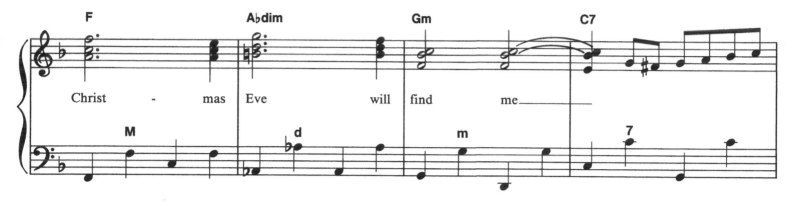

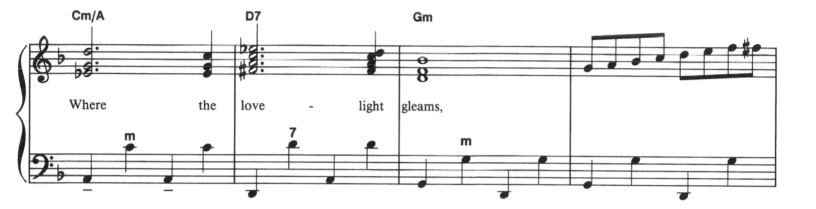

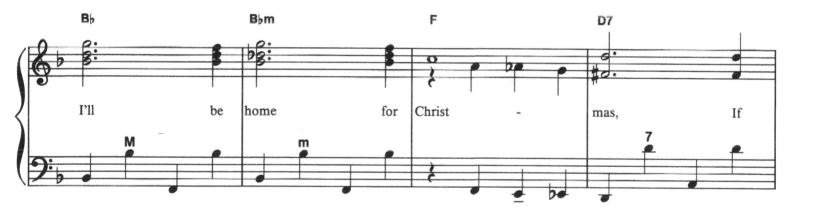

Jingle, Jingle, Jingle

Music and Lyrics by
Johnny Marks

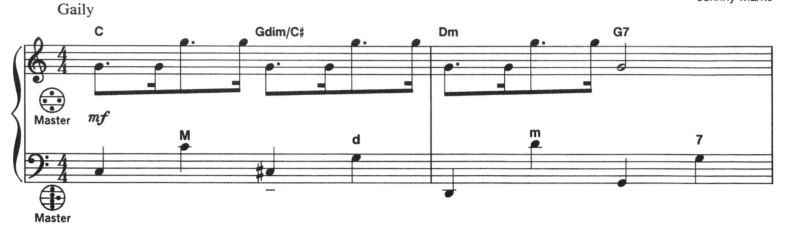

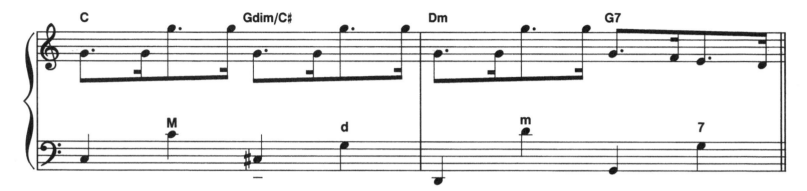

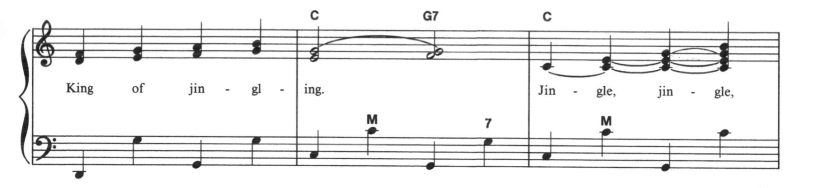

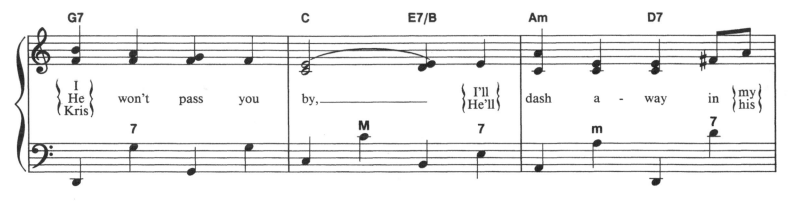

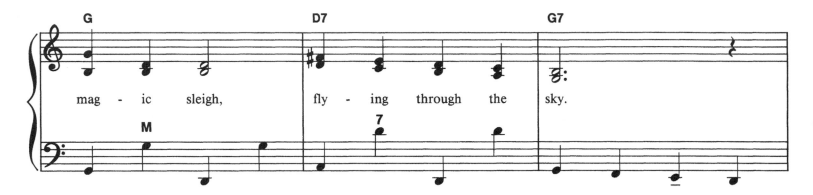

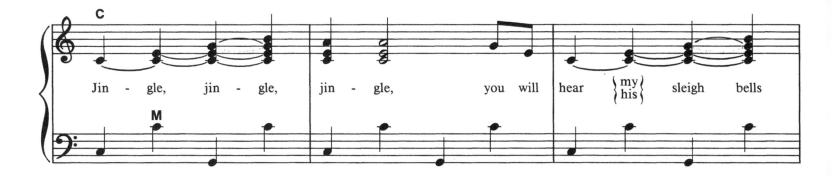

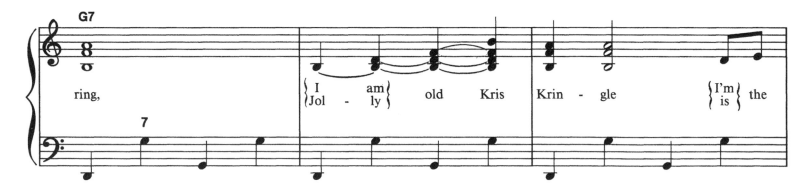

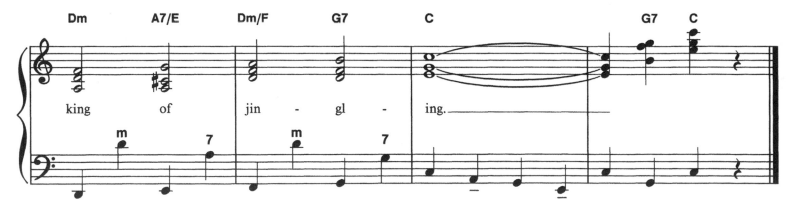

Pretty Paper

Words and Music by
Willie Nelson

Slowly, with expression

Crowd-ed streets, bus-y feet hus-tle by him.
Down-town shop-pers, Christ-mas is nigh.
There he sits all a-lone on the side-walk.

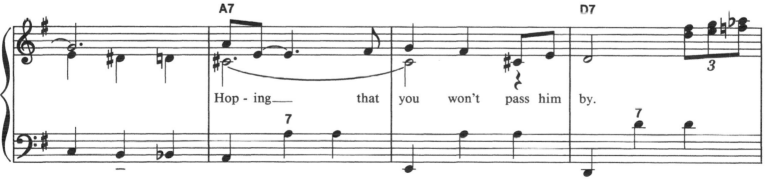

Hop-ing that you won't pass him by.

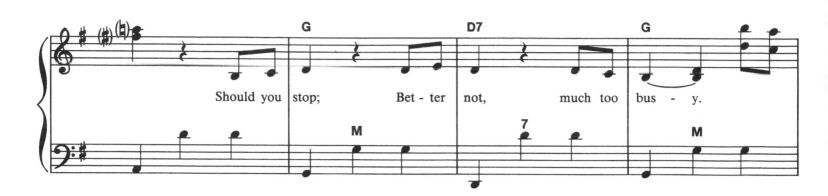

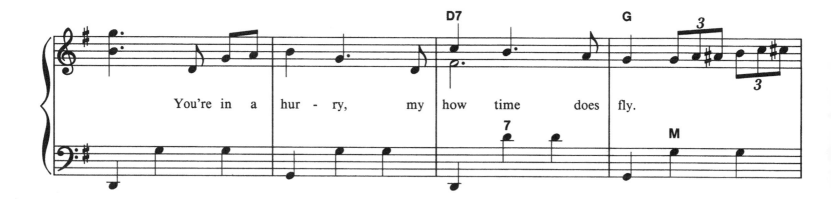

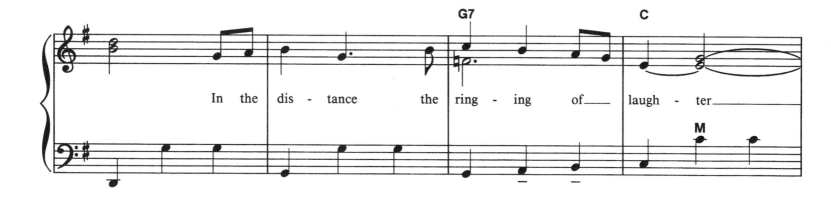

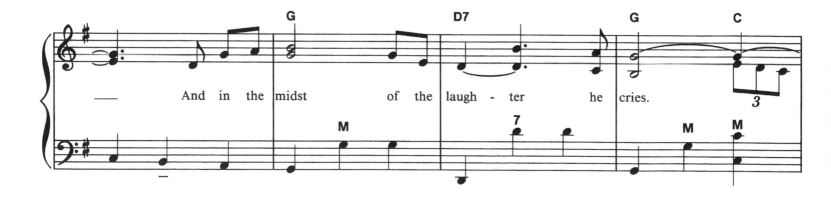

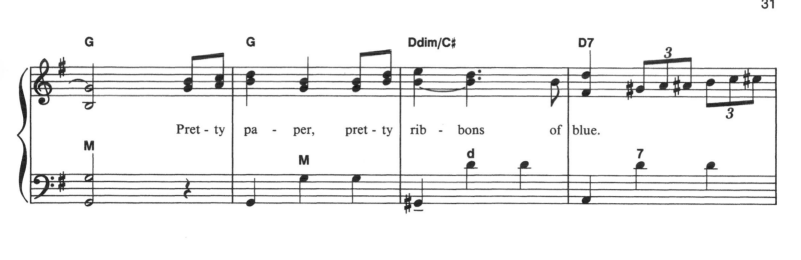

Pret - ty pa - per, pret - ty rib - bons of blue.

Wrap your pres - ents to your dar - ling from you. Pret - ty

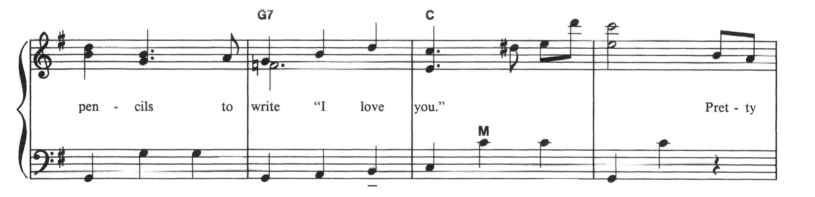

pen - cils to write "I love you." Pret - ty

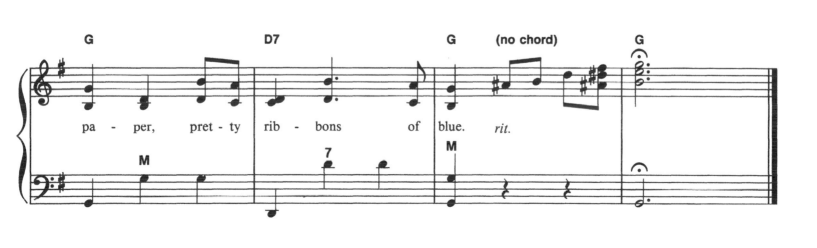

pa - per, pret - ty rib - bons of blue. *rit.*

Let It Snow! Let It Snow! Let It Snow!

Words by Sammy Cahn
Music by Jule Styne

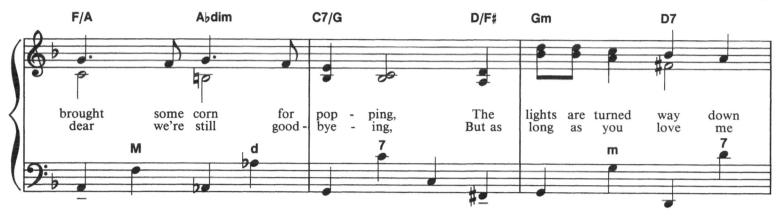

brought some corn for pop- ping, The
dear we're still good- bye -ing, But as

lights are turned way down
long as you love me

low.
so. } Let it snow! Let it snow! Let it snow! When we

fin - al - ly kiss good - night, How I'll hate go - ing out in the

storm! But if you'll real - ly hold me tight,

All the way home I'll be warm. The

snow!

A Marshmallow World

Words by Carl Sigman
Music by Peter De Rose

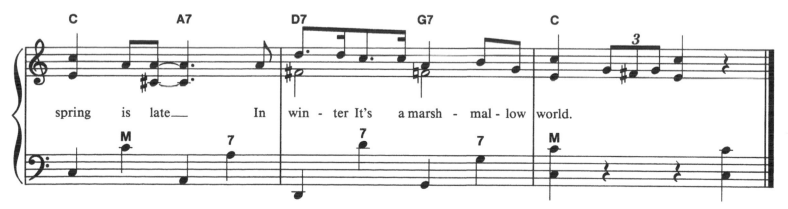

The Merry Christmas Polka

Words by Paul Francis Webster
Music by Sonny Burke

round and round the room we go, So get your-self a girl.

Now ev-'ry

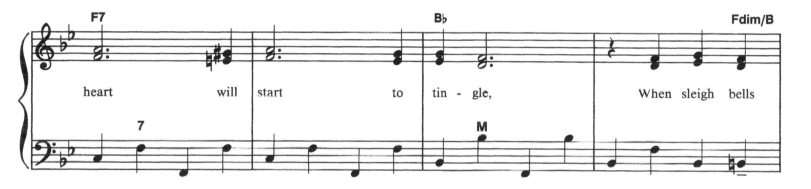

heart will start to tin - gle, When sleigh bells

jin - gle____ on San - ta's sleigh To - geth - er

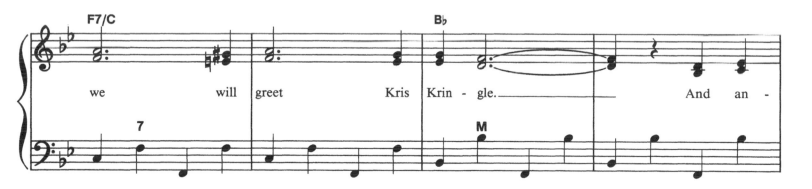

we will greet Kris Krin - gle.____ And an -

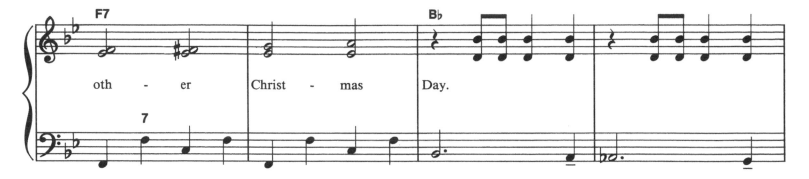

oth - er Christ - mas Day.

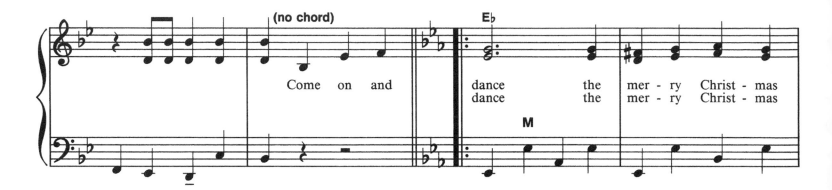

Come on and dance the mer - ry Christ - mas
dance the mer - ry Christ - mas

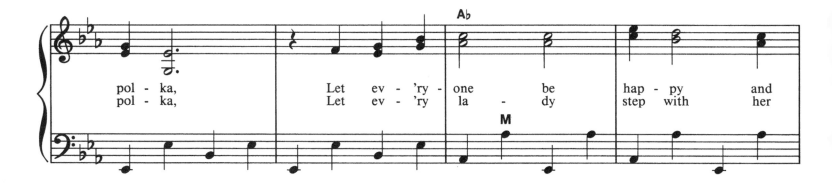

pol - ka, Let ev - 'ry - one be hap - py and
pol - ka, Let ev - 'ry la - dy step with her

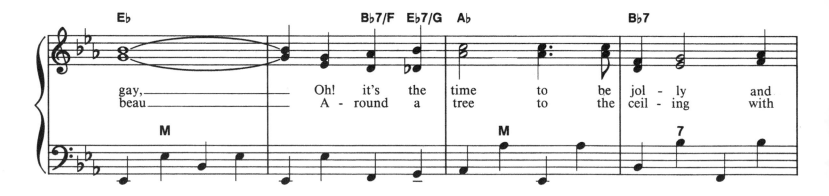

gay,___ Oh! it's the time to be jol - ly and
beau___ A - round a tree to the ceil - ing with

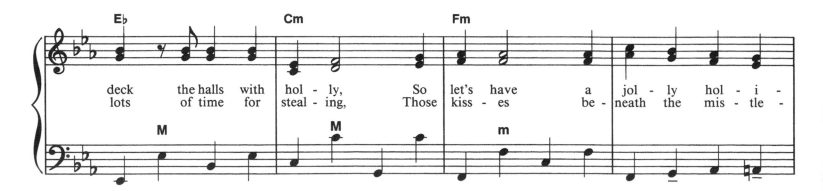

deck the halls with hol - ly, So let's have a jol - ly hol - i -
lots of time for steal - ing, Those kiss - es be - neath the mis - tle -

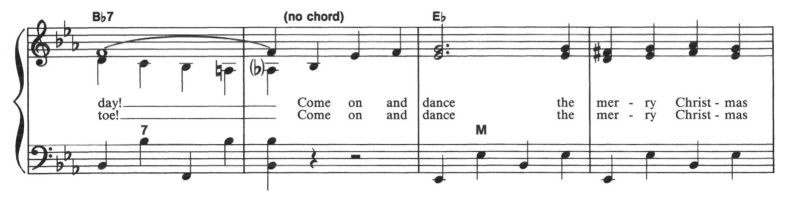

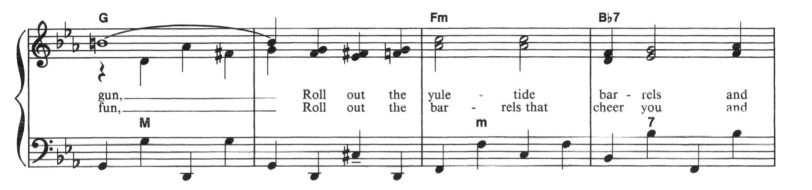

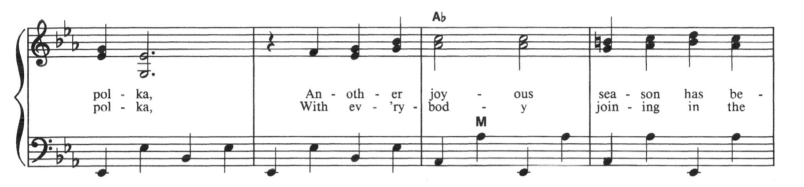

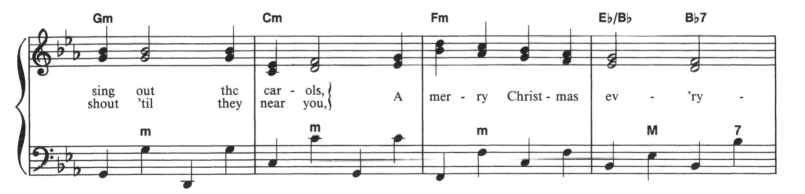

Rockin' Around The Christmas Tree

Music and Lyrics by
Johnny Marks

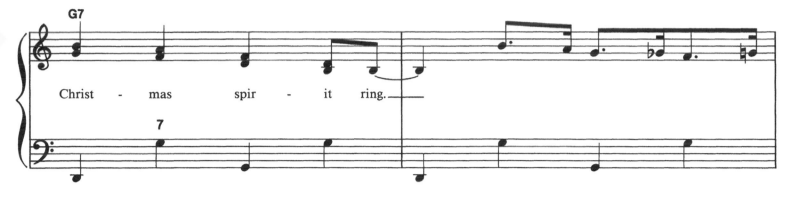

Christ - mas spir - it ring.

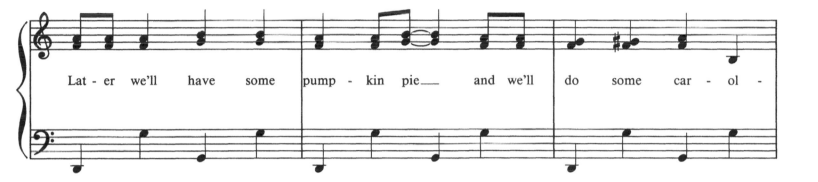

Lat - er we'll have some pump - kin pie__ and we'll do some car - ol -

ing. You will get a sen - ti - men - tal

feel - ing when you hear voic - es sing - ing,

42

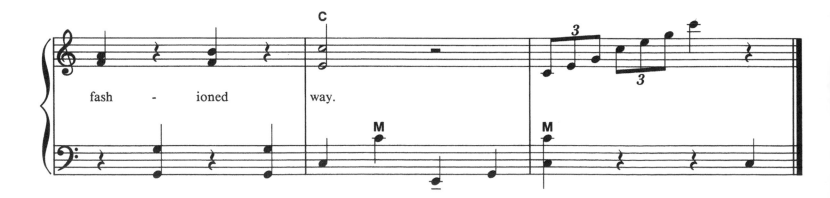

Rudolph The Red-Nosed Reindeer

Music and Lyrics by
Johnny Marks

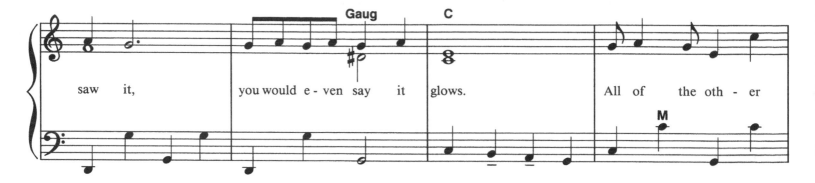

saw it, you would e-ven say it glows. All of the oth-er

rein - deer used to laugh and call him names,

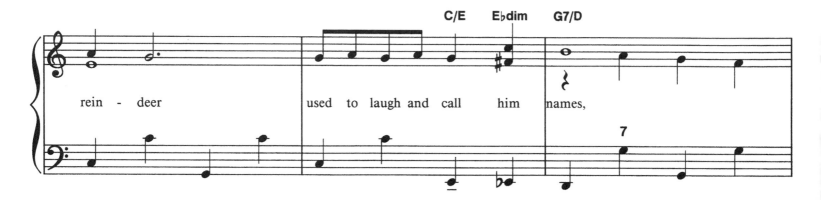

they nev - er let poor Ru - dolph join in an - y rein - deer

games. Then one fog - gy Christ - mas Eve,

San - ta came to say, "Ru - dolph, with your

Suzy Snowflake

Words and Music by
Sid Tepper and Roy Bennett

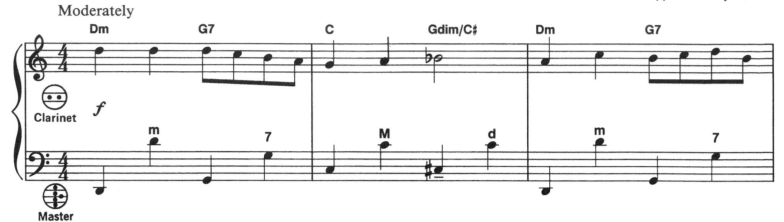

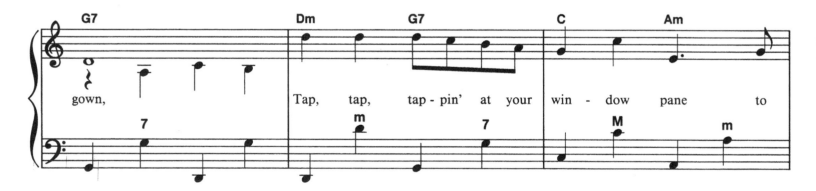

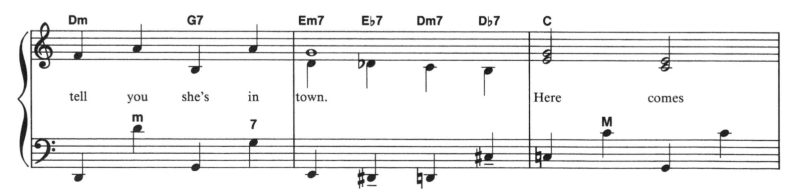

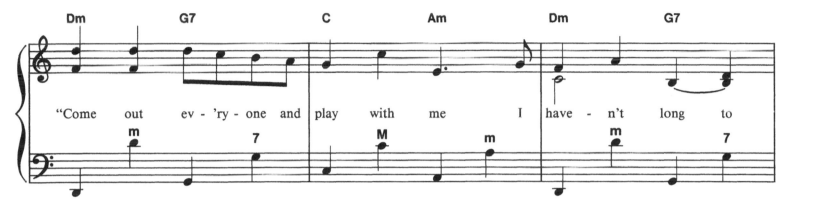

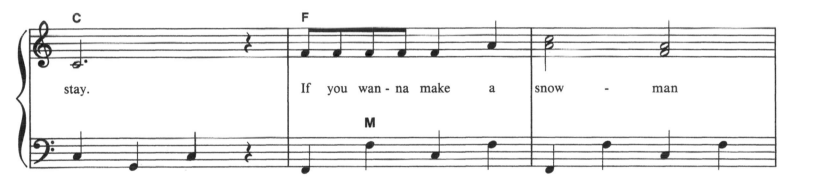

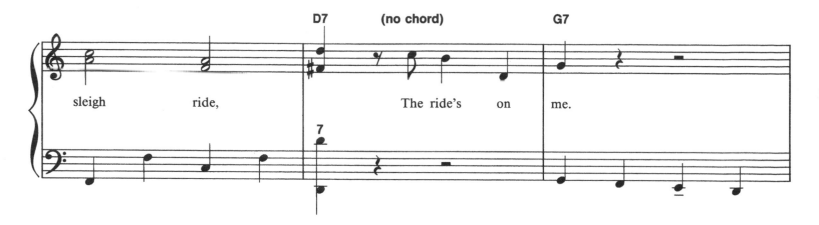

sleigh ride, The ride's on me.

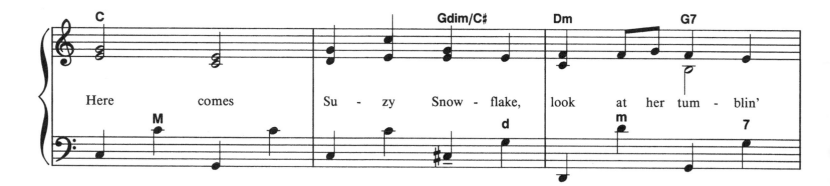

Here comes Su - zy Snow - flake, look at her tum - blin'

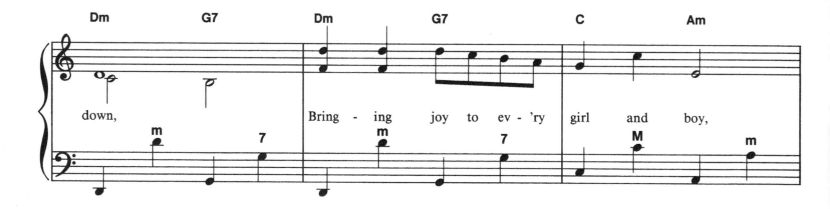

down, Bring - ing joy to ev - 'ry girl and boy,

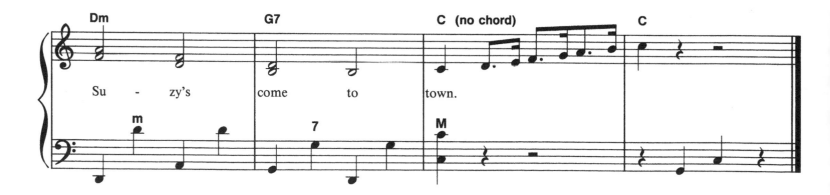

Su - zy's come to town.